Child/Home Early Language & Literacy Observation

CHELLO

CHELLO Tool

Observation Record

Name of provider(s): ______________________ Business name (if any): ______________

Name of observer: ______________________

Date, time, and duration of observation: ______________________

Hours of operation: ______________ Director: ______________________

Number of providers (e.g., providers, aides, enrichment personnel): ______________

Number of children with identified learning disabilities: ______ Number of English language learners: ______

Age range of all children in setting: ______________________

Primary language used by provider: ______________________ Primary language spoken in setting: ______________________

Languages spoken by children: ______________________

SECTIONS COMPLETED

- ☐ Literacy Environment Checklist
- ☐ Group/Family Observation
- ☐ Provider Interview
- ☐ CHELLO Tool Score Form

For the day of the observation

Total number of children: ______________ Number of girls: ______________ Number of boys: ______________

Ages of children observed (range in months from youngest to oldest): ______________________

General comments:

·P A U L·H·
BROOKES
PUBLISHING CO.®
is a registered trademark owned by
Paul H. Brookes Publishing Co., Inc.

To contact the publisher: Paul H. Brookes Publishing Co.,
Post Office Box 10624, Baltimore, Maryland 21285-0624
1-800-638-3775; 1-410-337-9580; fax: 1-410-337-8539
www.brookespublishing.com

The *Child/Home Early Language & Literacy Observation (CHELLO) Tool* is intended for one-time use only and can be purchased in packages of five (under ISBN-13: 978-1-55766-936-0). To order, contact Brookes Publishing Co.

For information on bulk sales, contact Brookes Publishing Co.'s Sales Manager at sales@brookespublishing.com, or call Brookes at one of the numbers listed above.

For information on arranging training for the CHELLO Tool, please contact Brookes Publishing Co.

Manufactured in the United States of America by
H&N Printing & Graphics, Timonium, Maryland.

Child/Home Early Language & Literacy Observation (CHELLO) Tool

by Susan B. Neuman, Ed.D., Julie Dwyer, Ed.M., & Serene Koh, M.A.

Literacy Environment Checklist

Group/Family Observation

Provider Interview

CHELLO Score Form

Literacy Environment Checklist

CHELLO

Examine the environment for the following elements. Make sure to read the helpful information in italics below many of the items. Circle the correct answer. The total score for each subsection is the sum of the individual items.

Book Area

1. Is an area set aside just for book reading?

	Dedicated book area	Area shared with other materials	No area
Circle one:	2	1	0

If there is no book area, move on to "Book Use."

2. Is the book area orderly and inviting?

	YES	NO
Circle one:	1	0

For example, are books organized and displayed on a bookshelf or bookcase?

3. Is the book area comfortable?

	YES	NO
Circle one:	1	0

For example, are there items such as pillows, cushions, or soft materials so that children can look at books comfortably?

4. Are books easily accessible to children?

	YES	NO
Circle one:	1	0

For example, can children reach books on their own, without adult assistance?

Book Area Total ______

Book Use

5. Are books located throughout the child care environment?

	YES	NO
Circle one:	1	0

For example, are books available in different sections of the space devoted to child care?

6. Do books range in difficulty level (corresponding to the ages of children in setting)?

	YES	NO
Circle one:	1	0

For example, is there a selection of board books, picture books, easy readers, and other books available to the children?

7. How would you describe the overall condition of the books?

	Excellent	Good	Poor
Circle one:	2	1	0

8. How many books are available to children?

	26+	16–25	15 or fewer
Circle one:	3	2	1

9. Are there books of different types (genres)?

	YES	NO
Circle one:	1	0

For example, are there informational books, storybooks, ABC books, predictable books, number books, realistic fiction, and so forth?

10. Are there other print resources available in the setting?

Circle one:	YES	NO
	1	0

For example, are there children's magazines, individual or group-created books, poems, and so forth?

Book Use Total ______

Writing Materials

11. Is an alphabet visible at children's eye level?

Circle one:	YES	NO
	1	0

12. Are there templates or tools to help children form letters?

Circle one:	YES	NO
	1	0

For example, are there alphabet stencils, sandpaper letters, rubber stamps, and so forth?

13. Is paper available for writing?

Circle one:	YES	NO
	1	0

14. Are writing tools available?

Circle one:	YES	NO
	1	0

For example, are there pens, pencils, markers, crayons, colored pencils, magnetic letters, rubber stamps, and so forth available to the children without adult assistance?

15. Is an area set up and available for children's writing?

Circle one:	YES	NO
	1	0

In order to score this item YES, there must be a designated area used solely for the purpose of writing.

16. Are there displays of children's writing in the setting?

Circle one:	YES	NO
	1	0

For example, are there samples of scribbling, "writing," invented spelling, and so forth?

Writing Materials Total ______

Toys

17. Are there cognitively stimulating toys in the setting?

Circle one:	YES	NO
	1	0

For example, are there blocks for building, a water/sand table, or clay?

18. Are there props to support sociodramatic play?

Circle one:	YES	NO
	1	0

For example, are dress-up clothes, hats, telephones, cash registers, and toys related to housekeeping provided?

19. Are there alphabet games and/or alphabet puzzles?

Circle one:	YES	NO
	1	0

Toys Total

Technology

20. Is there a working computer for children in the setting?

Circle one:	YES	NO
	1	0

21. Are there recorded books or stories available for children to listen to?

Circle one:	YES	NO
	1	0

These can include books or stories recorded or played on a record player, a CD player, a Walkman, an MP3 player, or a computer.

22. Is there other technology available that supports children's language and literacy?

Circle one:	YES	NO
	1	0

For example, are there educational videotapes or DVDs, such as Between the Lions?

Technology Total

CHELLO Group/Family Observation

For each lettered item, choose a score from 5 (exemplary) to 1 (deficient). Record your score for each item on the corresponding line to the right of the box. Add scores and divide by the total number of items to get an average score for the page.

Physical Environment for Learning

	5 Exemplary	4	3 Basic	2	1 Deficient	
1. Organization of the Environment	There is **strong** evidence of an intentional approach to the organization of the physical environment.		There is **some** evidence of an intentional approach to the organization of the physical environment.		There is **minimal** evidence of an intentional approach to the organization of the physical environment.	
Evidence: *Status and organization of furnishings, as well as observations of traffic flow, activities, and materials available to children*	*a. Environment is clean and in good repair, with adequate lighting, space, and temperature control.*		*a. Environment is mostly clean and in good repair, with adequate lighting, space, and temperature control.*		*a. Environment is not as clean as would be appropriate for children. Some furnishings may require repair, and lighting and temperature control are inadequate.*	___
	b. Environment is intentionally organized with cognitively stimulating interest areas that support language and literacy development.		*b. Environment is intentionally organized for the most part with cognitively stimulating interest areas that support language and literacy development.*		*b. Environment is not organized with cognitively stimulating interest areas that support language and literacy development.*	___
Notes:	*c. Furnishings are child oriented and age appropriate.*		*c. Some furnishings are child oriented and age appropriate.*		*c. Furnishings do not appear to be child oriented and age appropriate.*	___
	d. Space is available for children to engage in active learning and movement, as well as to use for quiet reflection and relaxation.		*d. Some reorganization of space may be needed to better allow children to engage in active learning and movement or to use for quiet reflection and relaxation.*		*d. The room may be too barren or crowded for children to engage in active learning and movement or to use for quiet reflection and relaxation.*	___

Average score: ______

	5 Exemplary	4	3 Basic	2	1 Deficient	
2. Materials in the Environment Evidence: *Organization and content of materials and room displays*	There is **strong** evidence of age-appropriate and stimulating materials and toys (e.g., books, dramatic play themes and props, art and modeling materials, tools for scientific investigation).		There is **some** evidence of age-appropriate and stimulating materials and toys (e.g., books, dramatic play themes and props, art and modeling materials, tools for scientific investigation).		There is **minimal** evidence of age-appropriate and stimulating materials and toys (e.g., books, dramatic play themes and props, art and modeling materials, tools for scientific investigation).	
Notes:	*a. Materials and toys support learning and creative explorations (e.g., toys and books for learning the alphabet, numbers, other educational materials).*		*a. Some materials and toys support learning and creative explorations.*		*a. Materials and toys do not support learning and creative explorations.*	___
	b. Materials and toys are grouped in ways to support and sustain children's engagement (e.g., writing table with markers, paper, pencils).		*b. Materials and toys are mostly grouped in ways to support and sustain children's engagement.*		*b. Materials and toys are not grouped in ways to support and sustain children's engagement.*	___
	c. There is sufficient variety of materials and toys to encourage child choice and initiative in the service of learning.		*c. There is some variety of materials and toys to encourage child choice and initiative in the service of learning.*		*c. There is minimal or no variety of materials and toys to encourage child choice and initiative in the service of learning.*	___
	d. Materials and toys are easily available to children		*d. Some materials and toys are easily available to children.*		*d. Materials and toys are not easily available to children.*	___

Average score: ______

CHELLO

Physical Environment for Learning

	5 Exemplary	4	3 Basic	2	1 Deficient	
3. Daily Schedule Evidence: *Written schedule, lesson plans, or observations of daily routines.* **Notes:**	There is **strong** evidence of a daily schedule that includes both structure and choice (i.e., both provider-initiated and child-initiated learning activities).		There is **some** evidence of a daily schedule that includes both structure and choice (i.e., both provider-initiated and child-initiated learning activities).		There is **minimal** evidence of a daily schedule that includes both structure and choice (i.e., both provider-initiated and child-initiated learning activities).	
	a. Activities and experiences are regularly planned to promote children's interest, engagement in learning, and conceptual development.		*a. Activities and experiences are occasionally planned to promote children's interest, engagement in learning, and conceptual development.*		*a. Activities and experiences are rarely or never planned to promote children's interest, engagement in learning, and conceptual development.*	___
	b. Activities and experiences are planned on the basis of children's individual needs and interest.		*b. Some activities and experiences are planned on the basis of children's individual needs and interest.*		*b. Minimal or no activities and experiences are planned on the basis of children's individual needs and interest. There are too many whole-group activities.*	___
	c. Sufficient time is available for children's self-directed activities and independent explorations (e.g., alone, with other children).		*c. Some time is available for children's self-directed activities. Some activities may be adult directed.*		*c. Little time is available for children's self-directed activities. There is a predominance of adult-directed activity.*	___

Average score: ______

	5 Exemplary	4	3 Basic	2	1 Deficient	
4. Adult Affect	There is **strong** evidence of attachment toward children.		There is **some** evidence of attachment toward children.		There is **minimal** evidence of attachment toward children.	
Evidence: *Interactions between provider and children*	*a. Provider knows each child well and designs activities based on individual children's interests, abilities, needs, and approaches to learning.*		*a. Provider knows each child fairly well. Some activities are designed based on individual children's interests, abilities, needs, and approaches to learning.*		*a. Provider does not seem to know each child well. Activities do not appear to be designed based on individual children's interests, abilities, needs, and approaches to learning.*	___
Notes:	*b. Provider regularly expresses positive feelings toward children (e.g., laughing, smiling).*		*b. Provider may appear to be passive toward children, distant, or unavailable.*		*b. Provider's manner may seem harsh or punitive.*	___
	c. Provider regularly brings each child's home culture and language into the shared culture of the setting, so that the children feel accepted and gain a sense of belonging.		*c. Provider occasionally brings each child's home culture and language into the shared culture of the setting, so that the children feel accepted and gain a sense of belonging.*		*c. Provider rarely or never brings each child's home culture and language into the shared culture of the setting.*	___

Average score: ____

CHELLO

Support for Learning

5. Adult–Child Language Interaction

Evidence:
Interactions between provider and children as well as interactions between children and children

	5 Exemplary	4	3 Basic	2	1 Deficient	
	There is **strong** evidence of positive adult–child interaction.		There is **some** evidence of positive adult–child interaction.		There is **minimal** evidence of positive adult–child interaction.	
a.	*Provider regularly encourages children's verbal interactions by asking questions, encouraging elaborations, and supporting continual exchanges.*		*Provider occasionally encourages children's verbal interactions.*		*Provider rarely or never encourages children's verbal interactions.*	___
b.	*Provider regularly gives children many opportunities to initiate and actively influence verbal exchanges.*		*Provider occasionally gives some opportunities for children to initiate and actively influence verbal exchanges.*		*Provider rarely or never gives opportunities for children to initiate and actively influence verbal exchanges.*	___
c.	*Provider regularly talks with children throughout the day, speaking clearly and listening to their responses.*		*Provider occasionally talks with children throughout the day. Responses to children may seem distracted at times.*		*Provider rarely or never talks to children except to give directions. Children's responses are received passively.*	___
d.	*Provider regularly participates with children in language information activities (e.g., inquiry lessons, storybook reading).*		*Provider occasionally participates with children in language information activities*		*Provider rarely or never participates with children in language information activities.*	___

Notes:

Average score:

	5 Exemplary	4	3 Basic	2	1 Deficient	
6. Management Strategies	There is **strong** evidence for creating a caring community of learners through positive management strategies.		There is **some** evidence for creating a caring community of learners through positive management strategies.		There is **minimal** evidence for creating a caring community of learners through positive management strategies.	
Evidence: *Interactions between provider and children concerning rules and routines and the nature of conflict resolution*	*a. Provider regularly sets clear expectations and establishes routines that encourage positive, constructive relationships with adults and other children.*		*a. Provider occasionally sets expectations about rules, and children appear to have some understanding of routines.*		*a. Provider rarely or never sets expectations about rules, and children appear to have limited understanding of routines.*	___
Notes:	*b. Provider regularly uses explanations to lead children toward peaceful, independent resolutions of conflict.*		*b. Provider occasionally uses explanations to lead children toward peaceful, independent resolutions of conflict. Provider may resolve conflicts for children without always explaining the reasons for doing so.*		*b. Provider rarely or never uses explanations to lead children toward peaceful, independent resolutions of conflict. Provider may use physical action to resolve conflict and this may be done in a harsh or arbitrary manner.*	___
	c. Provider regularly encourages children to use language to verbalize their feelings.		*c. Provider occasionally encourages children to use language to verbalize their feelings.*		*c. Provider rarely or never encourages children to use language to verbalize their feelings.*	___

Average score: ______

CHELLO

Adult Teaching Strategies

	5 Exemplary	4	3 Basic	2	1 Deficient	
7. Vocabulary Building	There is **strong** evidence of intentional language use for building vocabulary.		There is **some** evidence of intentional language use for building vocabulary.		There is **minimal** evidence of intentional language use for building vocabulary.	
Evidence: *Interaction between provider and children during learning activities*	*a. Provider regularly uses multiple activities to introduce new words and concepts to children.*		*a. Provider occasionally uses some activities to introduce new words and concepts to children.*		*a. Provider rarely or never uses activities to introduce new words and concepts to children.*	___
Notes:	*b. Provider regularly encourages children's use of language in play and activities by asking questions, making suggestions, posing problems, and providing new information as needed.*		*b. Provider occasionally encourages children's use of language in play and activities.*		*b. Provider rarely or never encourages children's use of language in play and activities.*	___
	c. Provider regularly engages children in representational thinking (e.g., by asking open-ended questions, by recalling events not immediately present).		*c. Provider occasionally engages children in representational thinking.*		*c. Provider rarely or never engages children in representational thinking.*	___

Average score: ______

	5 Exemplary	4	3 Basic	2	1 Deficient	
8. Responsive Strategies	There is **strong** evidence of positive responses to children's interests and activities.		There is **some** evidence of positive responses to children's interests and activities.		There is **minimal** evidence of positive responses to children's interests and activities.	
Evidence: *Responses to children's queries or requests*	*a. Provider regularly responds contingently to children's questions and queries in ways that support children's learning.*		*a. Provider occasionally responds contingently to questions that children ask, but answers do not appear to support children's activity.*		*a. Provider rarely or never responds to children's questions and queries, or dismisses them.*	___
Notes:	*b. Provider regularly uses verbal encouragement in ways that are genuine and related to an actual task or behavior (e.g., "Here, try to write your name").*		*b. Provider occasionally uses verbal encouragement in ways that are genuine but may not be related to an actual task or behavior (e.g., "You are so smart").*		*b. Provider rarely or never uses verbal encouragement related to an actual task or behavior.*	___
	c. Provider regularly acknowledges children's accomplishments or attempts with specific comments (e.g., "I see that you wrote your name in capital letters"; "I see you drew Mommy's face").		*c. Provider occasionally acknowledges children's accomplishments or attempts with specific comments*		*c. Provider rarely or never acknowledges children's accomplishments or attempts with specific comments.*	___

Average score: ____________

	5 Exemplary	4	3 Basic	2	1 Deficient	
9. Use of Print	There is **strong** evidence that print is used to support children's learning and development.		There is **some** evidence that print is used to support children's learning and development.		There is **minimal** evidence that print is used to support children's learning and development.	
Evidence: *Presence of print and its use in the environment*	*a. Provider uses print to label many parts of the environment (e.g., cubbies, drawers, shelves).*		*a. Provider uses print to label some parts of the environment.*		*a. There is no evidence of labeling in the environment.*	___
Notes:	*b. Play areas include many literacy-related props (e.g., books, notepads, recipes, dress-up clothes for postal worker).*		*b. Play areas include some literacy-related props.*		*b. Play areas do not include literacy-related props.*	___
	c. Print is regularly used for functional purposes throughout the enviroment (e.g., menus, schedule of activities, rules, word wall).		*c. Print is occasionally used for functional purposes throughout the environment.*		*c. Print is rarely or never used for functional purposes in the environment.*	___

Average score: ______

	5 Exemplary	4	3 Basic	2	1 Deficient	
10. Storybook/ Storytelling Activities Evidence: *Observation of storybook reading or storytelling events* **Notes:**	There is **strong** evidence of a daily interactive story reading routine that is coordinated with age-appropriate goals for children's language and literacy development.		There is **some** evidence of a daily interactive story reading routine that is coordinated with age-appropriate goals for children's language and literacy development.		There is **minimal** evidence of a daily interactive story reading routine that is coordinated with age-appropriate goals for children's language and literacy development.	
	a. Provider regularly plans for and reads interactively to children.		*a. Provider occasionally plans for and reads interactively to children.*		*a. Provider rarely or never plans for or reads interactively to children.*	___
	b. Provider regularly reads to children in various groupings (e.g., in a whole group, in small groups, individually).		*b. Provider occasionally reads to children in various groupings.*		*b. Provider rarely or never reads to children in various groupings.*	___
	c. Provider regularly offers children opportunities to hear a story at different times throughout the day based on children's interest.		*c. Provider occasionally offers to read to children throughout the day based on children's interest.*		*c. Provider rarely or never offers opportunities for children to hear stories throughout the day.*	___
	d. Provider regularly coordinates book-reading experiences with ongoing projects, interests, and activities.		*d. Provider occasionally coordinates book reading experiences with ongoing projects, interests, and activities.*		*d. Provider rarely or never reads books that match current projects, interests, or activities.*	___

Average score: ______

Adult Teaching Strategies

	5 Exemplary	4	3 Basic	2	1 Deficient	
11. Writing Activities (Drawing, Writing, Scribbling)	There is **strong** evidence of an intentional approach to children's writing that is coordinated with age-appropriate goals for children's language and literacy development.		There is **some** evidence of an intentional approach to children's writing that is coordinated with age-appropriate goals for children's language and literacy development.		There is **minimal** evidence of an intentional approach to children's writing that is coordinated with age-appropriate goals for children's language and literacy development.	
Evidence: *Observations of writing materials and opportunities for children and providers to be engaged in writing*	*a. Materials are easily available for children's writing.*		*a. Some materials are available for children's writing.*		*a. Materials are not available for children's writing.*	___
	b. Provider regularly facilitates children's writing development through modeling, demonstrating, and encouraging children's attempts to communicate through writing.		*b. Provider occasionally facilitates children's writing development through encouraging children's attempts to communicate through writing.*		*b. Provider rarely or never facilitates children's writing development.*	___
Notes:	*c. Provider regularly helps children, formally or informally, write their own names and other words, phrases, or sentences.*		*c. Provider occasionally helps children, formally or informally, write their own names and other words, phrases, or sentences.*		*c. Provider rarely or never helps children to formally or informally write their own names and words, phrases, or sentences.*	___

Average score:

	5 Exemplary	4	3 Basic	2	1 Deficient	
12. Monitoring Children's Progress	There is **strong** evidence of documentation for monitoring children's progress.		There is **some** evidence of documentation for monitoring children's progress.		There is **minimal** evidence of documentation for monitoring children's progress.	
Evidence: *Recognition of children's progress (through portfolios, documents, assessments, and anecdotal records)*	*a. Progress of individual children in areas of cognitive, social-emotional, and physical development is recorded regularly and maintained.*		*a. Progress of individual children in areas of cognitive, social-emotional, and physical development is occasionally recorded.*		*a. Progress of individual children in areas of cognitive, social-emotional, and physical development is rarely or never recorded.*	___
	b. Portfolios, assessments, or other methods of documentation are regularly used to monitor children's ongoing progress in language and literacy.		*b. Portfolios, assessments, or other methods of documentation are occasionally used to monitor children's ongoing progress in language and literacy.*		*b. Portfolios, assessments, or other methods of documentation are rarely or never used to monitor children's ongoing progress in language and literacy.*	___
Notes:	*c. Progress monitoring strategies (e.g., observations, documentation, portfolios) are regularly used to inform instruction to support children's individual growth and achievement in language and literacy.*		*c. Progress monitoring strategies are occasionally used to inform instruction to support children's individual growth and achievement in language and literacy.*		*c. Progress monitoring strategies are rarely or never used to inform instruction to support children's individual growth and achievement in language and literacy.*	___

Average score: ______

	5 Exemplary	4	3 Basic	2	1 Deficient	
13. Family Support and Interaction	There is **strong** evidence of parent involvement in children's language and literacy development.		There is **some** evidence of parent involvement in children's language and literacy development.		There is **minimal** evidence of parent involvement in children's language and literacy development.	
Evidence: *Contact information and communication with families*	*a. Provider regularly communicates with families about children's cognitive, social-emotional, and physical development.*		*a. Provider occasionally communicates with families about children's cognitive, social-emotional, and physical development.*		*a. Provider rarely or never communicates with families about children's cognitive, social-emotional, and physical development.*	___
Notes:	*b. Provider regularly provides strategies for promoting family activities that support children's language and literacy development.*		*b. Provider occasionally provides strategies for promoting family activities that support children's language and literacy development.*		*b. Provider rarely or never provides strategies for promoting family activities that support children's language and literacy development.*	___
	c. Provider keeps parents regularly informed on children's activities and interests in the setting.		*c. Provider occasionally keeps parents informed on children's activities and interests in the setting.*		*c. Provider rarely or never keeps parents informed on children's activities and interests in the setting.*	___

Average score: ______

An interview will help the observer score items on the Group/Family Observation that may not be observable in the environment. The interview takes about 10 minutes. Some of the questions have prompts suggested.

Tell me how you plan your schedule for the children. What kind of activities and experiences do you try to include in their daily schedule? Their weekly schedule?

*(**Related Group/Family Observation elements:** 3, 7, 9, 10, 11)*

Prompts: How do you address children's individual interests and needs, especially those of different ages? What does a typical day in your setting look like? How do you combine structured and unstructured time? How do you incorporate ongoing home activities (e.g., cooking, gardening) into learning activities for children? (If available, you may ask for a copy of the schedule.)

How do you focus on children's strengths and challenges in learning? How do you use this information to plan experiences that enhance children's language and literacy?

*(**Related Group/Family Observation elements:** 7, 8, 9, 10, 11)*

Prompts: What strategies have been most effective in getting to know the children well? What specific challenges have you faced when getting to know the children?

How do you view your role with the children? If you could use one word to describe your relationship with the children, what would that be?

(Related Group/Family Observation elements: 4, 5, 6, 8)

Prompts : Do you see your primary role as provider? Nurturer? Helper? Teacher? What special strengths do you bring to this role?

What kinds of learning opportunities do you provide for your multi-age children? How do you plan for children of different ages and developmental needs? What specific challenges does a multi-age group bring to your planning and scheduling?

(Related Group/Family Observation elements: 1, 2, 4, 5, 6, 8, 9, 10)

Prompts : Are there certain activities that you plan for with infants/toddlers? Preschoolers? School-age children?

How do you communicate with the children's families? What strategies do you use? What specific challenges have you faced when communicating with families?

(Related Group/Family Observation element: 13)

Prompts : In what ways do parents support the child's language and literacy development? (Ask for copies of newsletters, updates, or other information if available.)

How do you monitor children's ongoing progress in learning? What are some of the strategies you use to assess children's language and literacy?

(Related Group/Family Observation element: 12)

Prompts : What are some of the challenges you have faced with monitoring children's progress? (If the provider does not appear to monitor progress, you might ask, "Who is responsible for measuring children's ongoing progress? Do you communicate regularly with him or her?")

CHELLO Tool Score Form

Provider: ______________________________

Observer: ______________________________

Literacy Environment Checklist

How to score the Literacy Environment Checklist:

1. Transfer the scores calculated for each section of the Literacy Environment Checklist to the chart provided here.
2. Sum the scores from each section of the Literacy Environment Checklist to get a total score for this section of the CHELLO.

	Score
Book Area	
Book Use	
Writing Materials	
Toys	
Technology	
Literacy Environment Checklist score	/26

Group/Family Observation

How to calculate the Group/Family Observation score:

1. Transfer the scores calculated for each page of the Group/Family Observation to the chart provided here. Remember, the score for each page is an average of all of the individual items on that page.
2. Calculate a total for the Physical Environment for Learning, Support for Learning, and Adult Teaching Strategies sections by summing the scores for each section (i.e., Physical Environment for Learning subtotal = Organization of the Environment score + Materials in the Environment score + Daily Schedule score).
3. Calculate a total for the Group/Family Observation by summing the totals from the Physical Environment for Learning, Support for Learning, and Adult Teaching Strategies sections.

Physical Environment for Learning	Score
1. Organization of the Environment	
2. Materials in the Environment	
3. Daily Schedule	
Physical Environment for Learning subtotal	/15

Support for Learning	Score
4. Adult Affect	
5. Adult–Child Language Interaction	
6. Management Strategies	
Support for Learning subtotal	/15

Adult Teaching Strategies

	Score
7. Vocabulary Building	
8. Responsive Strategies	
9. Use of Print	
10. Storybook/Storytelling Activities	
11. Writing Activities	
12. Monitoring Children's Progress	
13. Family Support and Interaction	
Adult Teaching Strategies subtotal	/35
Group/Family Observation score	/65

Overall CHELLO Score

To calculate the overall CHELLO score, add the Literacy Environment Checklist score and the Group/Family Observation score together.

Overall CHELLO score	/91

CHELLO Tool Score Form: How to Interpret Scores

The following is a guide to help you interpret the scores this setting has earned on two different sections of the CHELLO: the Literacy Environment Checklist and the Group/Family Observation.

Literacy Environment Checklist

To use this chart, look at the score from the Literacy Environment Checklist section of the CHELLO. The highest score possible is 26, and the lowest score possible is 1.

Description	Score
Excellent	21–26
Fair	11–20
Poor	Below 11

Group/Family Observation

To use this chart, look at the total score from the Group/Family Observation section of the CHELLO. The highest score possible is 65, and the lowest score possible is 13.

Description	Score
Exemplary	55–65
Above average	44–54
Basic	33–43
Fair	22–32
Deficient	Below 21

ISBN-13: 978-1-55766-936-0
ISBN-10: 1-55766-936-8

· P A U L · H ·
BROOKES
PUBLISHING Co.

www.brookespublishing.com

Manufactured in the U.S.A.